SUCCESS : A STORY YOU WRITE, A DESTINY HE CREATES

RITIKA DEORA

Contents

Contents

Acknowledgements

I would like to thank three people who were like lifeblood to the publishing of this book. While one of them is my mentor,the other two are my batchmates. First of all, I would like to thank my two batchmates namely Iqura Memon and Keerthana Naidu for motivating me to pen down my thoughts and standing by my side all through the writing period of this book. Secondly, I would like to thank Mr. Ashok Mahajan, my mentor, for guiding me with editing suggestions and assisting in the publishing of this book.

Lastly and most inevitably, I would like to present my special thanks to my parents – Mr. Arun Deora and Mrs. Madhu Deora for providing me with the resources and environment to express my ideas without any hesitation.

FOREWORD

The aim of this book, my dear readers, is to make you realize the importance of not just knowing but learning. Each chapter in this book revolves around a lesson beginning with one of the 26 alphabets that English, as a language, provides us. This book will enable you to learn the significance of each letter in life. This book will compel you to learn the existence of several important things around you which you feel you lack, but you actually don't. This book will urge you to not to mesmerize the 26 alphabets of English as it is but to grab the potent learning it provides. Doing so, this book will ultimately prepare you to captivate success within you. However, to grab this most sought-after asset in life, you need to link all the pearls (in the form of the chapters of this book) in the most appropriate manner, and if you are able to do that, mind you, success is all yours.

My motivation to write this book while I was pursuing my grade 12th came not only from the domestic and school environment I got, but more dramatically from my curiosity – curiosity to learn new lessons (especially self-help and philosophical), curiosity to derive my own interpretations, and, curiosity to share my ideas with others.

Thus, I would like to say a sincere thanks to you for picking up this book and letting me calm down my curiosity of getting my ideas through to you. At the same time, I wish you a good luck for "exploring", "experiencing", and, "expressing" anything and everything in your life freely and fearlessly.

A Reality Check

Whether it is relationships or career, social life or personal life, business world or one's inner world; from east to west, from those who think sky is the limit to those who live in the underworld – everyone seeks something, isn't it? We desire, we fantasize, we dream of, we aim for something. Isn't it? Wait, what is it that we all look for? Money? A big "No". The answer's quite simple – it's Success, which often becomes Sucking. Does that mean I am claiming success as bad or not good? Again, a "No". It's just that we have got a blurred pair of glasses i.e., almost all of us allow our pair of eyes to have a glance at only the initial "SUC" of success and overlook what's beyond it-"CESS", which stands for process. In other words, most of us fail to enjoy the very elixir of success, which is the process itself, and hence, in due course of time, it becomes "sucking" instead of "success". However, the question on your platter would be: is this disease of blurred vision curable or uncurable? Well, to your surprise, this disease is chronic but curable anyway. To cure it is no doubt a challenge, but I want you to remember this: "Winners embrace challenges".

The coming chapters of this book unfold a series of steps, in the form of theories, that will enable you to unblur your vision and magnetize success thereby.

I

the theory of Almost and all

You might use the two words- “almost" and “all” interchangeably while speaking and writing. It’s no surprise, not a matter to worry about either. But Gals and Lads, the moment you interchange these two words in your life, you become more prone to the disease of blurring your sight and ultimately losing it beyond treatment. Let’s understand how.

You must have heard that most people, having walked nine hundred and ninety-nine miles along their odyssey to success, give up just a mile before they actually have it in their possession. Yes, you read it right – just a mile before. But wait, does that “just one extra mile” make even a slightest difference? Mind you, it’s a havoc in an individual’s control. Remember what the renowned American football coach Jimmy Johnson has said - “the difference between ordinary and extraordinary is that little extra”, and every successful person is extraordinary. More specifically – if you measure what's preceding and following this one extra mile on a weighing scale, you might end up observing the scale turning upside down, for we have on one hand the "all" and on other hand the "almost", which is equal to weighing everything against nothing. Sounds funny, right?

Let me put it this way - on a foggy morning, you might not be able to identify a signboard even from a meter's distance. But when you absolutely reach where the signboard is, not the thickest fog can prevent you from noticing the same. The key here is that a meter's distance is still a distance from your destination and can be equated to or merged with the destination under no circumstances. And, if considered so, it might lead to accidents for sure, as might be the case if you on a foggy morning assume from a meter's distance that there's no danger ahead.

To understand this analogy more clearly, imagine the moment when a hospitalized person who was about to die, actually dies. That single moment of transition, which is too minute to be measured even, is of immense significance though because when the person is about to die, he is still alive, but the moment he dies he is no more than a dead body. This fine line of transition between life and death, my dear readers, is a bridge between almost and all.

Conclusion

Never give up on attaining 99.9%, always look up to your absolute aim i.e., 100%. Never pause midway, keep heading at your own pace to the far end of that cliff where one actually takes off to reach the destiny of his choice. In yet another words, reaching the top second stair on the ladder of success is still a failure and not the success. So,

always attempt and keep on attempting to bring to the conclusion whatever you choose to begin. Don't leave off or put off anything you give a start even if it's at the verge of completion, for it still renders your work incomplete. Remember that if you elude to give the ultimatum of 100% to your work, success will elude you ever and ever again in your life, for there is nothing like trailer in real life – it's either a film of entire three hours or as good as nothing.

II

the theory of Belief

Do you believe in ghosts? If you don't, you would not be afraid of a dark and deserted place or a haunted house in an isolated piece of land, right? Exactly. Now give a thought to this – Do you believe in yourself? If you do, you won't be scared of challenges and failures throughout your life. Sounds ironical but, my dear readers, this is how the theory of belief works in real life.

Believing in oneself is the very first step to making your aspirations come true because if you don't believe in what you aspire, the creative medium of your subconscious mind won't ever be able to bring your thoughts and ideas and ambitions to reality, no matter however hard and fast you strive. This is what Dr. Joseph Murphy has tried to explain throughout his bestselling book named - "The Power of Your Subconscious Mind." In simplest words, everything you think can be a given a real face provided you invest a firm belief in it and manifest it in your subconscious mind on an everyday basis. Remember that whatever you feed to your subconscious mind regularly, gets impressed on your conscious mind which then has the power to turn it into a real-life experience. That is the reason why some eminent psychologists claim our subconscious mind to be a treasure house of infinite miraculous powers, for it has that capability to add a practical edge or rather a life to our dreams, our aspirations. Hence, I say – Feed your subconscious mind with seeds of belief, a firm belief in the truth of your aspirations. Say a few words of success to yourself not just today but every single day to come. To be truly enforceable, have faith in your success such that you can envision it, imagine it, feel it and experience it in the space of your mind each time you close your eyes. With such belief in your success, you see, you won't have to chase success but it will follow you.

To put it straightforward into your mind, whenever you find time for your aspiration just sit peacefully for a while. In those quiet moments, close your eyes and visualize your ambition with the eyes of your mind. Dive into your ambition and live it as if it were a reality. If you follow these steps precisely for a few minutes every day, believe me or not, you will soon incorporate your ambition in your actual life in a manner as subtle as your routinely chores.

Conclusion

To make your dreams come true in the outer world, begin by bringing it to reality in your inner world. Make sure you have enough room in your mind to picturize your ambitions in the peaceful moments set aside from your everyday hectic schedule. Gradually, gear up the process and try to live your aspiration on the screen of your mind. Mind you, if you take these steps in the exact manner, the next step will be taken by your mind to print your aspiration onto the canvas of reality.

III

the theory of Conflicting emotions

You must have faced a situation resembling a conflict between two or more of your emotions, many a times in your life. One such conflict might sound like this – wanting to take up challenges yet reluctant to step out of comfort zone. You all might be aware of the fact that the path to success comprises a lot many perplexities and embracing these is indeed essential in order to tighten your grip on success. Being aware of this fact, many of you might be ready and willing to take up challenges in life. However, willingness alone doesn't work. No doubt, the quote - "Where there is a will, there's a way" makes perfect sense and holds true in one's life, infact, willingness is like the very initial step or the stepping stone in the process of taking up difficulties. But, my dear readers, in order to be able to embrace these difficulties and make them melt like an ice-cream candy in scorching heat, you must and you will have to step out of your comfort zone. The key here is that as one can't witness both the faces of a coin at a given point of time, in a way too similar, one can't beat challenges being in his comfort zone. Mind you, the comfort zone referred to here is the "traditional comfort zone" where one believes that everything be served to him as simply and quickly as bed tea, and, where one equates success to material well-being and a luxurious lifestyle. This is the comfort zone that genuine, and not the so-called successful people, are known to have given up.

The irony or the actual conflict is that winners are the ones taking comfort in challenges itself. Yes, you read it right. Giving up your comfort zone, here, doesn't imply being out in scorching heat and toiling yourself with unnecessary tasks. It rather implies that you don't be guilty of missing out on the short-term gratification for attaining a huge one.It implies that you balance your emotions and relieve yourself of the guilt and anxiety and FOMO of losing – losing at least some momentary gain in order to receive another, because getting it all is not possible. It enables you to seek the infinite other doors open rather than whining for the one you have already shut. It enables you to look forward to challenges as a form of opportunities, and hence, rejuvenate in them. Being able to counter challenges thus requires not only the abandonment of your existing comfort zone but also its extension beyond the conventions of society. Believe me or not, if you extend the criteria or rather the scale of your comfort zone to challenges, you will be able to fight them invariably and effortlessly, in no time.

Conclusion

As a saying goes "if you try to control everything, you end up controlling nothing". In other words, getting it all without any sacrifice is not possible in the off-screen world. Thus, I say – instead of missing out on the success itself, put your momentary gratification or short-term pleasure on fire so as to be able to enjoy the warmth of a truly successful living. Don't give up your comfort zone but extend it to inculcate challenges invitingly and naturally. Having done this, you minimize the opportunity cost of success because then you see even challenges as a form of opportunities, thereby giving a soothing and comforting relief to your eyes, and not letting it weep however many perplexities carrying a log of pain cross your way.

IV

the theory of Diminishing success

You must have heard of a very famous law in economics, known as “the law of diminishing marginal utility”, given by the Prussian economist Herman Gossen. The law states that as one keeps on consuming more and more units of a commodity, the utility (satisfaction) derived from each successive unit declines because of the fact that the intensity to consume declines with increase in the number of units consumed of a commodity. In light of the same law, my dear readers, what relationship between time and success do you think fit? A similar law, which I call as “the law of diminishing success” establishes a link between time and intensity of success as well. The essence of success deteriorates with time provided the person concerned loses his thirst to learn more and more and more, and grow bigger and bigger and bigger. The very moment a successful person shows a red signal to his hunger for knowledge and curiosity, the law of diminishing success comes to play.

The great author Ashwin Sanghi has said in his book "The Sialkot Saga" - "dealing with success is sometimes harder than dealing with failure". This implies that not attaining but retaining success is much more a challenging task and at the same time, essential indeed to be truly successful in and throughout life. Mind you, as long as you keep your lust for learning alive, your success can be threatened by nobody. But as and when you lose it, you find your success in jeopardy. The key, my dear readers, thus lies in keeping your learning spirit awake day in and day out, and taking every pinch of knowledge that comes your way in any guise, any form, anytime and anyone from. Never take a step back from learning, never shy away from expressing your inquisitiveness, never hesitate to demand an answer and never cease to pose a question. An attempt to suppress curiosity is, metaphorically, an attempt to inhibit success in anything and everything you do.

Remember always that a truly successful person is one who all the time feels as if he were in kindergarten. He is the one who learns every time, applies his learnings every day, still urges and craves and hungers to learn more. He is the one who knows and agrees that there can be no end to the scope of learning- neither his age nor the hour of the day, neither the fact that he is already learned and successful nor the one that he already has a locker full of wealth in his cupboard.

Conclusion

A well-known dialogue goes like this: "people say taste the success once, tongue wants more". In line with the same

dialogue, I say – never stop craving for knowledge. Let you tongue taste it not once, not twice but ever and ever again, for the taste of knowledge brings with itself the flavor of success. Keep the candle of curiosity lit within your heart until it stops functioning. Let your inquisitiveness be alive so long as your mind and body and soul are. Never forget that as long as the learning spirit within you is awake, your success shines high and bright, and once this spirit dozes off, your success dims itself part by part until it fades to invisibility.

Make sure your learning spirit stands as firm as the old man did in Akbar's regime, standing the coldest of cold water, one entire night, inspired by a candle flame visible at the far end of the fort. This candle flame in your case, my dear readers, is the flame of enlightenment.

V

the theory of Experiments

If you have passed your grade 10th or grade 9th at least, you must have performed, say, minimum one experiment in the chemistry or physics lab of your school. And, if you are a furtherer in the stream, you must be performing these lab experiments every now and then, right? However, your answer to these questions doesn't, at all, matter here. Whether or not you have performed any experiment in a closed lab ever, till date we have done and till our death we will be doing several experiments in the arena of our life. This is what matters. Yes, you read it right. The experiments that we perform in our actual life and not necessarily in a confined lab area, is what really makes sense. No doubt, me, you and every single being on this earth experiments every single day but then, what makes successful people stand out from the crowd is that they value these experiments more than we do. Hence, they are the ones gaining most from these so-called every day, petty experiments. The lesson I want to convey here is - value your experiments. If you don't, why would or rather why should anyone else do? Remember always to respect your work, your actions, and, your experiments. Now, you might be confused why am I using the word "experiments" so often. My dear readers, don't take the word experiments in scientific sense. For more clarity, let me confess – I am not a person from science background but a typical commerce student (i hope that appeals). The oxford dictionary defines the word "experiment" in two aspects as follow:

1. To do a scientific experiment for proof
2. Try or test new ideas, methods, etc. To find out what effect they have

Mind you, the word "experiment" in this chapter is purely being used in its second meaning given above. Let me put forth the logic as well – life is uncertain and the "precise predictability quotient" in life is zero, i.e., we can never, with utmost accuracy, predict an outcome or guarantee as to what is going to happen the next minute, next hour, next day, next month, next year. In simple words, we don't go everyday by plans, we don't live every day in a planned manner, we can't plan everything from tip to toe a day prior. In short, some experiments are inevitable and each one of us is bound to perform it. Now let's dig deeper into the experiments performed by those who are known to have grabbed success in their lives. Successful people perform a wide variety of experiments. In other words, they try out everything on their own rather than believing or following someone else blindly. And then, they also value these experiments performed by them every now and then. This is what makes the true definition of experimenting and this is what we call experiential learning – learning by trying out, failing, and then trying out, and not simply going by what others ask you to do. However, it is also vital to understand that life is too short to experience everything in one's own life. It is said that life teaches us everything in the form of experience, but that doesn't necessarily imply one's own. Humans are smart enough to learn from others' experience as well, and if you choose to do so, you choose to learn, grow and shine beyond normal. Thus, one must be ready, willing and prepared to learn from others' experience as well. In this way, we can experience more, excel more and exceed others in terms of success.

Conclusion

Successful people never hesitate to explore new things, hence are they the inventors, innovators, influencers in the society. The gist of this chapter thus lies in the fact that in order to be successful, try it out yourself. Start experimenting and framing your own theories rather than accepting, in an uninquisitive manner, the theories proposed by others. Experiment, experience, examine and then draw your own conclusions. Wherever possible, learn from others' experiments as well, not indifferently but after examining the all ifs and buts, prefix and suffix, and, pros and cons of such experiment. So, what are you waiting for? Put on your lab coat and start experimenting, from today itself, in the lab of your life.

VI

the theory of Fulfilment

Who do you want to be successful in your life for? The most probable answers to this question would be – yourself, your family, your society, or, your mate. Whatever the case may be, being successful for any of the above four options will provide you a sense of happiness and fulfillment, right? And that is the reason you chose to be one, otherwise why would you be? Unfortunately, however, many people don't allow themselves to be fulfilled even after having chosen to be successful for their own selfish self. If that is the case, poor man, success is not desirable for you. You neither deserve to be one nor are you aware of its true meaning. While ascending the ladder of success, my dear readers, being fulfilled at each step is a must. Mind you, being fulfilled here doesn't imply that you be so satisfied as to feel that there's no need to go next level and consider where you stand today as the ultimate result. No, never. Success is a consistent process and you need to be persistent with it. It never ceases. In fact, if you try applying brake to it, you head in the opposite direction, towards failure. Thus, fulfillment here doesn't imply satisfaction and reluctancy to take a further step, but a consensus of your mind and soul to your striding forth in the direction you are currently facing. It implies that your mind and soul have given consent for you to move a stair more on the success stairway you are ascending. In other words, fulfillment implies that you are glad to be where you are and, at the same time, you are poised and mentally prepared to make more footfalls on the same track that you are walking up. And, if it is not so, you either made a wrong choice or you need to work out the direction you want to head in rather than putting your feet haphazardly on any tile around you.

The theory of fulfillment thus urges you to self-introspect a while before you jump to the next stair on your success stairway. Remember always that self-introspection is never a waste of time, it's rather an investment and, believe me or not, investment in time yields high and very high returns (though it takes its own time). In other words, before taking a tread forward on the rail of success, take a few moments of station. During this waiting period, however, don't sit idle. Pry your conscience every now and then, in an attempt to be able to understand if it wants you or not to further in your trek to the mount success.if it says a yes, ignite your passion and fasten the speed along your journey, and if it says a no, it's good, better and best that you have taken a timely decision of quitting your journey and thereby preventing yourself from the blunder awaiting you on the way.

Conclusion

Fulfillment to success is like fuel to vehicle. In order to drive yourself to success, follow the indications given by your conscience with regard to fulfillment. If your conscience says no, don't drive further for your vehicle is empty of fuel (i.e., fulfillment). On the other hand, if it says yes, burn your fuel more and gear up.

VII

the theory of Gardening

What comes to your mind when you hear the word "garden"? A stretch of lush green grass, rose bushes, and a variety of scented flowers beaming their beauty, all in perfect shape and size. What else? Don't worry. Even if you imagine this much it's pleasant and worthy enough, for growing even the grass in that perfect shape and size is quite a tough job. You need to nurture it – with all love and care, all knowledge and equipment, all time and effort, in order to call it a "garden". In a same fashion, my dear readers, you need to nurture your dreams – with all curiosity and confidence, all perseverance and persistence, all endurance and experience, to call it a "success". The key, my dear readers, is that success grows over time and it must keep growing, in the same fashion as a garden remains a garden only until it grows and is trimmed (i.e., shaped) on a regular basis. For the germination of success, you need a seed in the form of an idea, which comes from curiosity and unrestricted imagination. For the growth of your success over time, you need confidence, perseverance, persistence, and endurance in you and your ideas. And, to trim it and mould it in a perfect shape, you need to modify your efforts in accordance with the experience that you as well as the others have had in the past (application of experiential learning).it is only then that you will be able to generate not only quantitative but a qualitative success – as beautiful as the garden you imagined.

However, the most significant analogy between gardening and building success in life is that gardening requires you not to pour the entire can of water or a bagful of fertilizer at once but to allocate it as per time, quality, requirement and productivity, and so does success. The theory of gardening thus urges you to nurture you dreams like a gardener – with numerous resource and emotion, in an apt proportion; not just once or twice but ever and ever again, so that your garden of success remain.

Conclusion

Gardening is a job which many people love to take up as a hobby, while others claim as highly time and energy consuming. The beauty of this task but lies in the fact that it is time and energy consuming, because the hours and sweat that your garden is nurtured with makes its beauty seem more beautiful and the pleasure it provides feel more pleasant.

The process of gardening works, in the same fashion, in the world of success as well. If you nurture your dreams

like a true gardener, you give rise to a success garden which is strong, sustainable, beautiful, and bountiful.

VIII

the theory of Humor

Let me put your senses to work by posing to you an interesting question- when was the last time you laughed your heart out, with your mouth wide open and displaying almost the 16 pairs of your white teeth contrasting your body complexion? I have absolutely no idea whether or not it would be an easy task for you to trace back to that day but let me tell you, if want success to pay you a permanent visit and not just drop in and drop out, humor must be an inevitable part of your so-called hectic timetable. Mind you, humor is not concerned with laughing or chuckling or showcasing your teeth each time, on every silly matter. It rather refers to "amusement". It is, in simplest words, the art of making people, including your own self, happy and interested and spirited and lit up. It is the ability to comprehend the positive aspects of anything and everything, and then use it as a tool to keep oneself as well as others around amused. It is a behavioral or rather a personality trait that enables you to drive out negativity and captivate positivity in the arena of your mind. It not only involves laughing, giggling and joking but, most essentially, keeping an inviting smile on your face, and, excludes whining, saddening, discarding and disregarding. The key is - an exultant smile on your face acts as a green signal for success to come and embrace you. A mundane expression (without smile), on the other hand, is a red signal to success, for it makes your efforts look pseudo (fake) no matter how much toil and determination you take them with, thereby uninviting and disregarding success in your life.

Being humorous thus asks you to laugh off all your pains, fears, anxieties, stresses, depressions and other hampering emotions, and thereby open your mind up to the rays of constructive virtues like determination, dedication, curiosity, enthusiasm, zeal, and the feeling that "yes, I can do it and I will do it". By sucking the weeds of chaos and disheartenment out of your head, humor provides you the strength to embrace difficulties and, at the same time, allows space for the germination of success seeds. Thus, I say – taking time to laugh and make yourself happy is not a waste of time but a sheer and effortless move towards success.

Conclusion

An excellent sense of humor is a most essential feature of a truly successful person. It not only enables you to laugh off your pains and tensions but also provides strength to withstand challenges, thereby allowing spacefor the development of a success-oriented mindset. And then, as a saying goes: laughter is the best medicine; so why not pick

up this free medicine and a building block to success right now?

IX

the theory of Ideation

You must have heard people saying that imagining or fantasizing is a characteristic of an idle or rather a foolish person, for ideation, in their opinion fetches nothing in real life. I agree with what people say, partly. No doubt, mere ideation doesn't produce any fruit. However, my dear readers, you must not fail to pay attention to the fact that even the greatest of great works begin with just an idea, or more precisely, "imagination". The clothes that you wear, the various commodities you use throughout your day, the delicious cuisine you munch, and even the extraordinary scientific inventions that exist around us had once, in the untraceable abyss of time been imagined by someone, somewhere before bringing it unto reality. Ever since the inception of humanity, there has been an inception of ideas, and people have given a shape to their imagination in the form of films and books which we call as "fiction". If you trace all such fictional books and movies, you would discover that most of the so-called modern and technologically advanced inventions that we see around us today have had been in the creative imagination of artists (writers, filmmakers, painters) long back. Several prominent inventions, for instance submarine, cell phone, helicopter, rocket, etc. are all inspired by sci-fi novels and films namely Jules Verne's novel "twenty thousand leagues under the sea", american television series "star trek", Jules Verne's "clipper of the clouds" and "war of the worlds" written by H.G Wells respectively, and more such works of science and fiction till date continue to inspire thousands of inventions like driverless cars, hover bikes, etc. But for the imagination and fancy of these artists, we would not have been able to witness the present greatness of science and it is not a matter of surprise to say that the seemingly unrealistic and too good to be possible inventions that we come across in sci-fi movies today might surround us tomorrow in real life. Thus, sincere thanks to all the imaginers who have ever imagined a new reality.

Now comes the interesting question – would you like to be one of these imaginers I just thanked? Obviously yes, but how? Quite simple. Just don't curtail the freedom of your creative mind. Allow it to wander wherever and whenever it wants to. Provide it with space for creativity and it will provide you with all the success without even being asked. Nourish your mind with a few moments of relaxation every day, make sure to empty it of all sorts of thoughts and let it wander around. It is only then that creativity will invade your mind and working on that creativity will bring you, sooner or later, the success that you seek.

For more clarity, let's take the example of a painter. What do you think makes him give birth to the masterpieces of art? Imagination. Could you think of any other answer? Some of you might say "emotions" such as love, pain, joy, dolefulness, etc. Undoubtedly, emotions induce a painter to paint, but then, how would he give these emotions a form without imagination? Just think about it.

What William Blake has said in the opening lines of his poem "auguries of innocence" is what I call the most important sign of a successful person:

"to see a world in a grain of sand
And a heaven in a wild flower
Hold infinity in the palm of your hand
And eternity in an hour"

Conclusion

The whole and soul of this chapter is – imagine, idealize and imbibe, for without it you can never aim, act or achieve success in life. Imagination has the power to bring to reality that which seems impossible. Imagination, my dear readers, is the only way to know that tomorrow can be different from today, that a better version of reality exists, that there is something new which is unexplored till date. And when you explore that newness in common everyday life, which no one else does, you discover yourself at the top of the success stairway.

X

the theory of Jogging

How would you feel about having a jog in the chilled morning airs of a nearby park one summer dawn while the sun shines bright and cool, sweet breeze blowing through your face and flowers on the verge of blooming? I don't think it would be wrong to assume that one would be much desiring to experience such a jog. Well, to your pleasant surprise, a jog is what even success demands from you. Yes, you read it right. The path of success requires you keep heading towards your goals at a gentle pace as while one jogs. It demands persistence and continuance in your efforts and eagerness to harness your goals. It asks you to ensure that your blood remains warm and burns like a fire-cracker but doesn't cool down or freeze like ice at any point of time. It asks you not to wait and watch like those who are called cold blooded but to soak your hands and feet and body into the sweatful warmth of uninterrupted jogging towards your destination. It requires you to neither to slow down nor to rush through your odyssey, but to pace forward steadily and gradually, like a simple jog. It requires you to experience and enjoy the process bit by bit, to its fullest. It wants you to be firm and consistent through all the plateaus and hills and troughs and ditches in the journey, through all the ups and downs that come your way, through all the blind turns you face, and through each and every phase of moon you see – whether a first quarter, a full moon, a waxing crescent or no moon at all. It wants you to take the roller coaster ride of success with as calmness and readiness as one undertakes a morning jog. It asks you not to turn downhearted when finding yourself in a ditch and not to climb on cloud nine while discovering yourself on one among the numerous hilltops along your way to success. It demands you to face the boom and the crises alike, with nominal mood swings and without extraordinary sentiments. It demands you to be disheartened at no time and exultant at all times, including the time of downfall or what we call recession in economics. It wants you to carry that one simple, sober and sweet smile on your face throughout your voyage to success, which you keep on the same face while jogging. It asks you to face everything you find along the way as invariably and inevitably as you encounter your friends or known ones while jogging. It asks you to dive into the environment of success as gracefully as you enjoy the weather- whether cold or warm, pleasant or unpleasant, while jogging. It wants you to take efforts genuinely and steadily still effortlessly. It asks you to breathe in the air of stress at times but to exhale it as well, as one does while jogging- breathing in and breathing out in perfect time. It asks you to work or rather sweat but relax at the same time.

Conclusion

Success is a process that closely resembles jogging, in the sense that it never asks you to come after it recklessly and hastily, or let your blood cool down either. It asks you to be consistent – to pace forward continuously without a break, still, at a pace that allows to enjoy the journey and not just rush through it.

It requires you to relax in your work itself, to not to overburden or underestimate yourself, to breathe in the air of stress sometimes but to exhale it as well, to accept everything that comes your way with a smile; all in a manner as you do while you are on a jog and not a job. If you consider your job as a jog, you see, you will effortlessly take all the efforts to reach the height of success you seek.

XI

the theory of Kriss-kross

You must have played crossword, word search, sudoku or any such sort of a crisscross puzzle in your childhood. And if yes, you must have, undoubtedly, enjoyed it. But the question that this chapter is concerned with is – how many of you play and enjoy playing crisscross or krisskross off-paper? In other words, how many of you play and enjoy playing it with people rather than numbers or words? Whether you have played or not such krisskross till now in your life, you must begin playing it after you complete this chapter. This game of krisskross that humans play among themselves, in today's business-oriented world, is known as networking, and, you need not necessarily be a businessman to be able to play this game. In fact, to become a successful businessman or any other successman, you must possess the mastery of this skill. While the word "networking" was initially seen as a cliché term associated with computer science and gradually got to a wide use in business and marketing sense; today it is one among the several mantras to attain success in any field. The key, my dear readers, is that you never know your turning point in life. You never know where and who the life-changing idea in your life be inspired from. Thus, during the course of hunting for the turning point in your life, don't miss to familiarize and interact with as many people as you can, for you never know who amongst them can be a source the transformation in you and your life, or, can plant a seed of success in your mind. Talking and interacting and communicating and discussing is, therefore, never a waste of time. This is how you build network, a huge network, a network which can act as an inspiration for your success story as well as an audience to read out your story to.

In simpler words, the bigger the network you have, the wider the range of ideas you are exposed to, and hence, more prone are you to making something great out of the many little ideas you get – internally as well as externally. It is not just that interacting with others provide you an exposure to others' ideas, but it also enables you to know the depth of your own ideas which you earlier didn't scale. Thus, whenever and wherever you find people, don't hesitate to approach them with an inbuilt curiosity to grab all what they have to provide you with. Talk to them naturally and then gradually begin to include more interesting or relevant ideas into the conversation. Try to get the maximum out of the conversation, for you don't know which particular line can turn out to be an inspiration or impetus or insight for you to begin with your success story. And, if the people you approached really proved a help, or, you could prove a help to them, don't lose the line of contact. Be in touch and make them a part of your permanent "success network". If and when you come across experienced personalities, make a note of the important lessons they offer you from their past and when you chance upon inexperienced personas, jot down the fresh ideas they open your mind to. Make sure that you make their ideas a part of your notebook, and, both of them a part of your network. Remember always that a person like-minded as well as a person not like-minded with you qualifies to be a part of your network. While a like-minded person motivates you to work on your idea and offers you similar ideas so as to widen the scope of your success, a person not like-minded presents you with criticism which acts as an insight in to the areas of improvement you need, thereby helping redefine and refine your scope of success. On the yet another hand, if you find a person who you could prove a help to in his success, don't forget to give him a place in your network, for his success then forms a part of your success as well. In this fashion, my dear readers, if you go on building your network (including all the five categories of people), you see, this network will, one day, turn out to be your success network – radiating your success everywhere.

Conclusion

Whether or not you play a crisscross game on paper, do play a krisskross game, I.e., networking game in your off-paper life. Interact with as many people – younger or elder to you, less qualified or more qualified than you, like-minded or not like-minded with you; as you can. Converse with them, discuss with them, build new ideas with them. Maybe, one of these ideas can be the pillar for you to erect the enormous building of your success on.

Never hesitate to communicate, for a simple communication is the starting point for every great discussion, and, it is among these great discussions that

you can get a kick-start for your success story. Always be inviting to all kinds of thoughts, ideas, opinions and criticisms from all sorts of people, and those who offer any of these should be a part of your network. Don't forget that the network you generate today is an audience for you share your story tomorrow.

XII

the theory of Lifting yourself up

How many of you have clapped in dark and solitude, when the hall is empty and no one performing on the stage before your eyes, when you are the solo performer and you only are the evaluator? Taking a little time and effort to undertake this, my dear readers, you applaud none but your own self and it is indeed a prerequisite for you before you turn the lights on to discover a bountiful audience sitting comfortably in the armed chairs of that exquisitely scented, air-conditioned hall - laughing, giggling, clapping and cheering you out there on the stage, rather than a rabble of empty seats making the place look unappealingly deserted. In simple words, whether or not someone regards your success, you do. Prize your success, honor your success, love your success, sing your success, however small it be. Applaud yourself for every little undertaking that takes you forward in life and prevents you from advancing in the backward or unfavorable direction. Recognition is damn necessary and it is you who must recognize it. Award yourself a trophy, if need be, but make sure it's not left unrecognized.

Let me put you through another question – ever wondered why dreams don't come to you unless you sleep? Prior to answering this, try recollecting if you ever sought them after or beckon them with open eyes. If you didn't, they are not bound to come at any hour of the day except for night. But, if you did, they would come to you – in morning, at noon, in evening and at night, even if you don't close your eyes. Thus, what is necessary on your part is to dare–dare to dream with open eyes, dare to write your own story (no matter how society expects you to write), dare to listen to your own story, and, dare to love, prize and honor your story.

The key, my dear readers, is that if you don't, why would someone else lift you up? If you don't, why would someone else look up to you? If you don't, why would someone else prize your success story? If you don't dare to step in, why would the elevator take you to the topmost floor?

Conclusion

Success is a result of a thousand little steps, and, each step is significant if only recognized, not by the externals but the one undertaking them. Whether or not others pay heed to your success, is not a matter of concern. If you do, it's worth everyone else. Thus, the key is to exalt yourself, to appreciate your own efforts, and, to award a trophy to none but "you" for what you consider to be an achievement in your life, no matter the world's opinions or rankings.

XIII

the theory of Money measurement

If you have ever studied accounts in your life, you would know that there is a concept in accounting principles and standards, known as the "money measurement concept". It states that only the events or transactions that can be expressed or measured in terms of money should be recorded in the books of accounts, and that money value of transactions is what determines the success of business. This concept, however, holds good only in the world of accounting. In practical life, my dear readers, success cannot be accounted for purely on the basis of money. Many a times or rather most of the times, we do consider people with tons of money as successful but that doesn't make it necessary for them to be one in their own lives. The relationship between money and success can be defined as follow:

"money may follow success but success never chases money."

For instance, whenever an enlightened entrepreneur or any innovator launches a new product or brings a new idea into the market, it doesn't take off instantly or fetch him barrels of profits at once. But the moment his innovation enters the market, it does create an impact by revolutionizing the minds of people around and that is what marks the success for an entrepreneur, regardless of where his bottom line stands. In quite a similar way, if a person is able to make bucket full of revenue from his father's and grandfather's business which has been continuing for years, it doesn't mark the milestone of success in his life unless there was a value-addition to business on his part which enabled him to earn the same.

The key is, my dear readers, if you measure success on the scale of money you might experience a bullet train ride for a few years of your life but the everlasting or sustainable success won't be able to penetrate its footprints in your life. Thus, to call it a real success, one must measure it on the ground of inner peace, satisfaction and admirability or sobriety of life (which may or may not be luxurious) rather than on the basis of material wealth one can showcase the world.

Conclusion

Money is important to maintain books of accounts, to maintain bank balance, to retain property papers and to retain an enterprise. However, money is not at all a requirement to attain, maintain or retain success in life. Money doesn't mark success and success is not symbolized by it. Hence, it is advisable that you work for success and

money will come alongside (though it may take its own time). If you work for the money itself, success is never guaranteed for it never seeks nor accompanies money, it is the money that follows success. In other words, if you work for the attainment of true success in life, you will never ever fall short of money, though you may or may not have ample of it.

XIV

the theory of Narcissism

I used to wonder how she thinks about me. I used to wonder how he thinks about me. I used to wonder how he, she and they all, out there in that hugely huge world think about a person called "me". I never knew if another world existed where my tininess would at least be visible or rather be dominating. Today that I know, the reality is different, way too different- I wonder and I only wonder how I think of myself. I wonder where would I place myself in a row when there are two, three, four and infinitely many "me" fighting with one another, within myself. initially I wondered if such a world with only "me" in it existed, but presently I know that it exists and it is known as one's "inner world". I know this because I am a narcissist and I also know that narcissism is what has brought me exactly where I stand today. Now let's talk about you – are you aware of the inner world I just mentioned above? if not, let me tell you where you lag. To know the existence of your "me world", you need to know yourself, you need to be obsessed with yourself, you need to be in love with yourself. You need to challenge yourself; you need to compete with yourself, you need to defeat and win over your former self again and again and again. You need to listen to the others around you, to the people you believe in but ultimately, you need to follow only and only what your own heart says. You need to remember forever that the success story which begins with you, no matter how long it goes, how well it goes, how many people it comprises and how many resources it utilizes, but it ends with you, on you, and only you. You need to forget never the fact that you cannot spell "success" without "u".

The key is, my dear readers, the trophy of success requires you to run your own race. it urges you to establish your own standards of day and night, your own rules of in and out, your own policies of yes and no, and, your own discipline of right and wrong. it asks you never to fall in your own eyes. it says that it's okay to fall in others' eyes but not your own because when that happens, your soul turns hollow and you can't attain nor retain success with a hollow soul.

in other words, to be successful you need to be a narcissist; which, in my opinion, is person with this panchtatva – self-love, self-obsession, self-confidence, self-reliance and selflessness at the same time. While self-love and self-obsession enable you to explore your own self, and, trace the hidden caliber you possess, and, discover the treasure house of power within you; self-confidence and self-reliance encourage you to expose your potential to the world flawlessly and effectively. On yet another hand, selflessness ensures that you don't end up hating everybody or anybody else while loving your own self. it doesn't allow you to work for your selfish interests without regarding or giving back anything to the society. Thus, if you inculcate these 5 s in yourself, you insert a sustainable success in your life.

Conclusion

Narcissism asks you to love, respect, regard and rely on you own self while making sure that you don't harm or disregard the society either. it demands you to go by your own principles rather than following somebody else recklessly. it requires you idealize and simultaneously compete with your own self. it says that he who runs his own race is like the slow and steady tortoise who carries away the victory against a quick and clever hare who is known to have won among crowds.

XV

the theory of Odds to favor

Do you think the track that successful people march along is filled with roses? It is rather one with a few roses and as many thorns as innumerable. In other words, you will encounter perplexities all through your way to success and in the same fashion will you discover opportunities as well. However, you will simply pass these opportunities by if you don't know the art of odds to favor. This is because these opportunities won't come your way in a guise you expect them to. One needs to have an eagle's eye to identify and grab these blessings in disguise. Do you have that eye? If not, let's develop it by learning the art of, precisely called, "odds to favor".

The art of "odds to favor" requires you to contemplate upon and not let go of the difficulties you face along your way to your destiny. As i aforesaid, the path of success comprises many a thorn and quite a few roses, thus it is among these painful thorns that you may find some of the most delicate opportunities and once you are able to identify them, will you get the pleasure of stepping onto a rose. In other words, it is not that you will get a favor but you will have to convert the odds (symbolized by thorns) to your favor (symbolized by roses). In order to achieve this conversion, you need to follow these steps:

1. Contemplating upon each and every situation you face along your way
2. Listing out all the possible ways in which you can respond to the situation on a paper.
3. Critically analyzing each and every response and its likely outcome
4. Noting the results and selecting the best way to respond

As you incorporate the third step, you will realize that out of all the possibilities listed, at least 50% turn out to be positive in some respect. Remember, being able to minimize adversity is itself constructive. Thus, weigh each outcome on the scale of positivity and then choose the one which radiates maximum positivity which is equivalent to bearing minimum loss. Following this approach in life, you see, you will be able to claim that every difficulty has a positive facet. If it's not absolutely in terms of attaining an advantage over the other party or the situation itself, you can at least gain an advantage over your own self by subjecting yourself to the minimum harm. Metaphorically, if you don't get to get the exact gratification of stepping onto a rose, relieving yourself of the pain of chancing upon a thorn is still an option and worth being opted for. In yet simple terms, reducing harm is synonymous to creating good. Thus, go for it whenever and wherever you can.

Conclusion

Keeping in view the fact that everything has a positive angle to it, if you follow the four steps provided in this chapter for each perplexity you find your way, you will undoubtedly be able to get all odds to your favor (if not absolute gain over the situation, a relative gain over yourself). Hence, you see, your path to success will automatically get paved with the passage of time. However, a point to be kept in mind is that you must not rush with the above procedure. Adequate time should be put in to analyze the outcomes accurately and it is only then that you will be able to not only eliminate quite a many thorn that lie before you but also transform some of them to roses or any fragrant flower you choose to pick.

XVI

the theory of Perception

How would you define a one-liter glass containing water only till 500ml mark and not up to the brim – confused? Let's look at the possibilities. You could either say the glass is "half filled" or you could even say the glass is "half empty". Which one's not correct? None. Both the facts are undoubtedly true, it is just that they are stated using different words.and, a change in words doesn't necessarily imply a change in meaning. As to say, it is not a mandate for you to go by the conventional definition of success. It's not required that you chase what the chaps around you are chasing. It's not appreciable that you look at success in a frame that society wants you to, without giving it your own angle. In other words, success is not an absolute but a relative concept. There is no universal definition of success and there can't be framed one, for what is success for you might not be the same for others and vice-versa.if the people about you run after money, claiming it as success, you need not, and, in fact, you must not follow the same track blindly. You must have your own discretion as to "what is success". To be truly successful, you must take a distinct path, set original goals and work towards it in your own style, independent of the society. If you do so, my dear readers, you will be successful for sure, neither once nor twice, neither sooner nor later, but every time and everywhere in life. You will then be a winner in your own life, irrespective of whetheror not society claims it as such, for everyone has a separate pair of eyes to look at success in the frame he wants to. It is not at all a matter of concern if society terms your success as success. If you do, it's worthy enough. Perceive success in the way you want, be successful for what you consider as "success" in "your life". Achieve success for the ones who deserve to be a part of it – yourself, your family, and the society that you form (not the one that tries to form you). Define yourself and your success, in your own terms, before others do in their own.don't attach tags to success, for it itself is a tag that needs no explanation. Don't associate success to a specific event or target or persona but to yourself, so that you automatically be successful in whatever you do, however you do.

Conclusion

The aim of your life should be "success" and not what society defines it to be. Remember always that you have got that pair of eyes which no one else has, and you have the sole right to use it for what you seek to look at and not what others ask you to. Today, right now, form your own definition of success based on your terms, your desires, your destiny.

XVII

the theory of Quantification

How many hours did you sleep last night? I guess five, six or maybe ten? Okay, so at what time did you sleep exactly...did you sleep peacefully or were you provided with disturbance? First of all, don't be tensed by so many questions at a time. Quality and not the quantity of sleep matters, is what i am trying to convey. Similarly, what all have you quantified in your life? Studies, satisfaction, happiness, relationships, friends, working hours, number of chapatis or dosas or burgers or pani -puri or anything you eat? Just give it a thought- is it really the quantity and not the quality of all the above mentioned or unmentioned elements that matter in one's life? I would say, it's just the opposite way round. For instance, let's say you study six hours a day and one of your friend studies just two hours a day with twice or thrice the level of determination. Who do you think would be able to produce better results? If you get to choose, which option do you think is more desirable and preferrable? On the ground of logical as well as statistical reasoning, second option is worth being opted for. This is not only because of the hiked-up level of determination your friend has in the second case but also because the four hours of spare time that your friend gets and you don't, may be used by him to relax his mind and soul thereby boosting his determination level up so that he turns out to be even more productive next time. In simpler words, taking time to prepare yourself for work is in itself more productive than exhausting yourself with a continued high dose of work without being aware of its futility. The point i want to get through to you is this - don't bind yourself with certain number of hours of work to be able to achieve your true goal in life. Being workaholic is not what success asks for. No doubt, it may help you at times to climb the stairway of success but is not a commendable formula for the same. The formula i believe in is somewhat similar to the very first chapter of this book "the theory of almost and all". I keep it simple and straightforward as follow:

"work with 100% determination or don't work at all. When you do, do it to the fullest and when you don't, just don't."

In bollywood, there's a movie called "qayamat se qayamat tak". In terms of attaining success, i say, it's like - "from determination to determination". The moment your determination comes to an end, there comes a full stop to your possibility of being successful as well. In that case, my dear readers, the number of hours of hard work you had put in, is rendered absolutely in vain. Thus, you must work on your determination rather than quantifying the hours of work, for the work you do with so high a determination is itself worth a hundred hours of work. However, what i am trying to emphasize here is the dominating power of determination over the number of hours you work, in terms of effectiveness and quality of work. This doesn't imply that one should go by mood swings rather than work requirements. The chief idea here is that determination is the key to success. If you are determined to do something or you get the nerve to do something, just go for it without any second thought. On the other hand, if you lack determination, work first to build it up for without it no matter how many hours you work, its futile.

Conclusion

Quality and quantity are two words that sound almost same but are not actually identical. They are rather like two faces of a coin, i.e., impossible to get both at a time. Thus, I say, unlike a simple coin with heads and tails, keep this coin a little biased towards "quality" for quality and not the quantity is what takes you to great heights. The simplest test to this phenomenon is your sleep. Try out the following two steps at your home:

1. **Sleeping at 1' o clock in night and waking up at 1' o clock in the noon next day**
2. **Sleeping at 10' o clock in night and waking up at 4' o clock in the morning next day**

Having experienced both the scenarios in my life, I would say, the difference in the energy and motivation levels in the above two situations is beyond one's imagination. In quite a same manner, my dear readers, working for a little time with high level of determination produces a thousand times commendable results than working for hours with want of it. Besides, you see, when

you are determined, more working hours don't exhaust you but when you are not, even a few make you fatigue stricken. Thus, if you get tired more while working less, just take a break, leaving what you are working on and resume it only when it is vice-versa. On the other hand, if you feel all the more concentrated and not exhausted while working, just keep on carrying forward your work without glancing at your watch.

XVIII

the theory of Regrets

You must have, for something or the other, often regretted in your life, right? You must have, after having made a decision, often thought: "was it worth it", and, "should have I done it"? Even I have, but must we? Holding regrets is one of the major effects as well as causes of failure in life. Yes, my dear readers, you read it right. It isn't just that failures lead to regrets but regrets lead to another failure as well. This cycle of failures and regrets continues to go on like what we call "the vicious cycle of poverty" in economics, wherein we say that a poor man is poor because he is poor, i.e., poverty leads to poverty and so on.

Let me ask you another very interesting question – have you read the poem called "the road not taken" by robert frost? If not, let me brief you. The poem talks about how it feels to make a choice when several different options are available, how it is to take a road when two or more appear in front of your eyes, how it hurts to not to be able to experience both the faces of a coin simultaneously. In any of the above cases, you might regret while you opt for one, leaving another alternative, thinking that the one which you didn't choose must be better. However, in reality, it may turn out to be worse or even worst. So, what's the use of regretting? Give it a thought.

We only make positive and pleasant assumptions regarding the alternative not opted for, and exactly the antithesis opinions for the road we actually walk on. We fantasize the road not taken in dark, without knowing where it exactly leads to. Hence, I say, rather than shooting in dark, why not illuminate the path you are currently treading on? The key is, my dear readers, never hold on to regrets in life. Don't give your time away to what you don't have the power to change. Rather, give it a "way". Invest it. Invest it in something which you possess the power to modify, to transform, and to make your destiny. Remember always to think before deciding, and not to, once it's decided; for thinking after deciding leads to regrets and regrets, my dear readers, does no good than bringing down your confidence for taking further decisions. Regrets are like a turbid liquid which enters your mind on your will and once you permit its entrance, you block your mind to the upcoming possibilities, and it is only when you do away with this liquid that you unblur the vision of your mind and open it up to the far-reaching possibilities of success in life.

Conclusion

Never carry the load of regrets in life, for if you do, you are too full to pick up opportunities on the way. Don't forget to empty your vessel of all sorts of regrets before setting out on your expedition to success so that it is open to all the

good it can find along the way because my dear readers, sooner or later, it is only good that follows bad, and you can't know the extent of its goodness or rather greatness unless you pick it up and put it in your vessel.

XIX

the theory of Small start

People say that in order to be successful, dream big. I say, in order to be successful, "dream big and start small." An addition of just two words "start small" brings about a huge difference in what most people believe and what I personally think. The point I want to convey is that a small start is complementary and not contradictory to your big dreams. Dreaming big is no doubt a prerequisite but it is those small, little steps that count for a stunning success in life, for without them your big dreams, however enormous they be, will always be dreams only. As it is said - "little drops of water make a mighty ocean", I say "little steps of endurance fill your success basket". Thus, never hesitate to take small, little, seemingly unimportant steps in your life because sooner or later, someday, somehow, it is these small steps that will fetch you a remarkable success by filling your basket bit by bit, ultimately up to the brim. Never forget that an airplane or even a rocket which flies so high up in and above the sky takes off from the same land that we stand on. The key is, my dear readers, your journey to the top end of the universe or even beyond that must begin at some point located on the earth itself. In other words, whether you aim to make it up to the Mount Everest or walk down the depths of the pacific ocean, you will still have to start from a point on the surface of the ground right beneath your feet. That point might not look that visible, that gigantic, that worth recognizing as the height of the highest mountain peak in the world, yet this point marks the onset of your success story. Remember that it is not the end but the very first move to achieve your end and mind you, it isn't just worth undertaking but worth remembering for your entire lifetime.

Whether your first step be small or very small or nearly invisible, it's still worth it for you could never take the second, third and all subsequent steps to success in its absence. For instance, as a matter of fact, all of us – you, me and anyone who is called a human, was born as a kid on this planet earth. Do you even remember what size were you when you were just born? Whatever your absolute size in inches be, but I am quite sure it would be less, way too less than your present size when you are holding this book in your hands. This is what is actually the crux of this entire chapter. My dear readers, as you have grown from a kid to quite a matured guy, from a few inched to full length (approximately) over the years, from your first day of landing to the present day; success, in quite a similar manner, germinates as a tiny seed, pushing itself to growth for years and years to become a full-fledged tree with fruits laden and flowers blooming all day and night, provided you nurture it with all the resources it asks for consistently and persistently.

Conclusion

The focal point of this chapter is that success is a seed and it is indeed essential for you to ensure that it grows gradually and continually and nutritiously, and doesn't erupt like a weed from an unknown and undesirable source, bound to be chopped off for the sake of survival if not growth at least. Remember always to start from the scratch, begin like a naïve kid, take off from the very ground below your feet to fly one day, cutting through the clouds and dyeing them in the color of your success.

XX

the theory of Thriving

Let's start with one of my favorite riddles – there are two individuals, one who has completed his twenty and another who has attained his forty. If I ask you who is more successful among the two, what and how would you answer? Most of you, I guess, would select the man with age forty for the answer, which, in my opinion, would be the answer if and only if he thrived in the forty years of his life as animatedly as the younger one in twenty years of his life. The key is, my dear readers, living and thriving in your success every moment is important. Never think that you will be successful, think that you are successful. Let success be contained in your blood and flow through your veins all over the body. Feel success in you, through you, all around you. Live each moment so successfully that you effortlessly become successful in whatever you do. Don't see success as the ultimate destination to be achieved, rather let it be the name of each tile that you pass by on your way and that you keep your feet on. Let success form a part of each station, each turn, each peak and each trough in your journey. If people around declare that you are successful but you don't live as such, you are only one in the eyes of the society and not in your own life.

Success is an unending process and you need to live this process every moment to claim yourself as successful. No doubt, success requires you to plan your future persistently and appropriately, and reflect upon your past actions and reactions to act as a guide, but the essence of success lies in the moment at hand. How successfully you behave and carry yourself today is a matter of utmost significance and can't afford negligence. Thus, inculcating success in your personality is a must. The key, my dear readers, is that – not just the end but means is important, not just the destination but the entire path marched along is important, not just the final product but the ingredients used is important, neither the input nor the output but the entire process went through is the most important as to say that neither the starting nor the ending point but the entire roller coaster ride is the actual amusement.

Conclusion

Many great personalities have said – work hardwith determination and success is all yours. I agree. But, in the process of working hard, harder and hardest, don't forget to live your success in every single effort you take because if you do, all your efforts, however hard they be, are rendered lifeless and that can never add success to your life. As much as sugar is essential to make a dessert taste actually sweet, living or rather diving in your success each moment is necessary to make you successful in life. In yet

another words, embracing the success straight to your heart and not just holding it in a bowl is important.

XXI

the theory of Unanimous satisfaction

Humans are the most social species on this planet, right? Have you ever wondered why is it claimed so? Mind you, it's because we can't live even a single day absolutely on our own. Not convinced? Just think – how many days can you live without food (that your mom used to cook), in an unclean room (which your maid used to clean), without talking to or reading or watching anyone (either on your mobile screen or physically present before you)? Can you imagine the existence of a life of that sort? Even if you can, I am quite sure you never experienced it nor would you want to. In the same manner, my dear readers, can you imagine yourself standing on the top edge of success ladder with support and sympathy of none? If one can't survive, one can't be successful all alone either, for coordination and not competition is the key to success. In other words, if not the circumstances and the people you encounter along your way fall in agreement or harmony with your aspirations, you can never get to the top most or even the second top most stair of success stairway. Thus, it is essential that you bring all these forces in harmony once again when you discover yourself at the far end of the stairway you are ascending. Remember always to be grateful to each and every being that you chance upon through your journey for being how they have been and thereby paving, in their own way, your way to success. It is only then that you will be able to generate unanimous satisfaction, once and for all. As it is said that knowledge, when imparted, multiplies itself; success, when involves more people, radiates itself brighter and to every nook and corner. Hence, unanimous satisfaction is not only advisable, but a duty of each and every successful person towards the society where he lives, grows and meets with success. Everyone who becomes a part of your expedition to success, must be given a share, even if the smallest, in your attained success as well, for unanimous satisfaction ennobles your success. No doubt, one sets out on his voyage to success all alone and crosses the finish line alone as well, but without those little contributions of numerous people on the way, crossing the finish line is more or less an unfulfilled fantasy. No doubt, one must be successful for oneself and not with the objective of being one in the eyes of the society, but, my dear readers, when you make society a part of it, you see, your success becomes more righteous, more welcoming and more echoing. It then enhances the thrill of your success experience. It then makes your success flag more vibrant and visible. It then makes your success a part of not only your own story, but the story of one and all. True winners are thus the ones not just converting failures and challenges to success, but, success to unanimous satisfaction, i.e., success for one and all.

Conclusion

As many little drops make a mighty ocean, many different people pave your way to success. Thus, to make your success sound, sober, and sustainable, you need to maximize the unanimity of the satisfaction resulting from it. The best way to do so is to acknowledge the all the little and huge contributors to your success, not merely by thanksgiving but by offering them a true place in your success story. Never ever forget the point you begin from, the path you walk on, and the people you pass by, for life is like a crossroad – the ones you come across on your way to success might come across you on their way to success as well. No doubt, you must stand out from the crowd and create your own identity, but going against the grain each time and looking down upon your fellows might cost you a lot in the long run. Thus, being social animals and an inevitable part of society, one must never forget the universal law of being unanimously successful and being unanimously served.

XXII

the theory of Volunteering

You want to be successful in the coming years of your life and that is the reason you are holding this book at the moment, right? But mind you, if you think reading this book will serve you all the many opportunities for being successful on your platter or will secretly attract success in your quiver one silent night, you need to either correct your mindset a little or rather drop the idea of reading this book any further because what I am going to advice you in this chapter might have annoyed you in your life till date, after testing your patience for quite a bit of time. This indispensable element in your expedition to success is known as "volunteering". In simple and confined terms, volunteering implies rendering a task without being asked or compelled for. However, in a much broader and success-oriented terms, it means taking the lead to initiate something purposeful without concerning oneself as to who will join hands in the initiative and when. It implies embracing an idea, implementing it, continuing through it and quitting it on your own discretion, without being troubled by the fact that you are alone. Remember always that one needs to set out on his odyssey to success all alone. Undoubtedly, several many people will join you along your journey, but at the end of the day they will leave you the same way. They might guide you, advice you, and prove helpful to you at times. Some of them might even be hurtful, harmful, distracting and destructive. But then, you must be less concerned about who passes you, joins you, disturbs you or leaves you either. In fact, even if you are engaged in a joint task where you have a team ready alongside you to help you out, you can't base your spirit and devotion to work upon the spirit and devotion of your team members. In other words, you must not be furious if anyone puts in lesser efforts or that with a lower extent of determination than you.

In order to turn out to be a good volunteer, you need to keep your working spirit up all through, without giving a thought to comparing it with others and modifying it accordingly. You need to remember always the quote given by William Johnsen: "if it is to be, it is up to me." Developing this attitude, you see, you qualify to become an excellent volunteer and a winner, my dear readers, is in first place, an excellent volunteer.

Conclusion

The essence of volunteering thus lies in the fact that you initiate and continue working your best towards your destiny with the same passion, equal amount of determination, and an indomitable will to succeed, no matter what appeals to the others working or not working

with you. Just imagine, if each member of a team would work in such a manner to succeed individually first, who can ever prevent the team to succeed collectively one day? Mind you, individual success in this context doesn't imply being self-centered all the time and attempting to attain success at the cost of your team. It rather means that collective success begins with individual success and that if one is defeated by oneself, he can contribute no good to the team. And, if you are the only one in your team, it's all right, you would succeed even sooner.

XXIII

the theory of When, Where and What

You must be, many a times in your life, wondering that in order to be successful, when, where and what should one begin with? A single answer to all these frequently asked questions is, in my opinion, "live in the moment". To elaborate, one must start where one is standing today, one must begin right now, and one must do what is best possible at the moment in hand. To know when to begin, you need to follow the element called "time" independently and impartially. If time asks you to relax at the moment, don't panic yourself unnecessarily and just be relaxed. If time, however, asks you to work on something, devote your entire self- your mind, body and soul to that work. Now, the question is – how do we know what time wants us to do at the moment in hand? The answer is "your conscience". Time has, my dear readers, a wonderful chemistry with one's conscience. Time and conscience, the two boundless, intangible forces that stretch to infinity are not mutually exclusive but go exactly hand in hand. In other words, whatever your conscience asks you to do at any given time, is what the time itself demands. The key here is that one must be connected with oneself enough to be able to comprehend this "call of conscience". One can do this by, as I aforesaid, living in the moment. If you practice the art of "living in the moment", you see, you effortlessly follow the call of your conscience every moment that passes by. Living in the moment doesn't just imply accepting your present, it is rather concerned with inviting your present with open arms, rejoicing in it, and being able to identify the best opportunities it provides. I remarked in the beginning of this chapter that in order to be successful you must perform what is best possible at the moment. And, to discover the best contained in any moment, you need to live it to the fullest. That is why I say – living in the moment is an art and this art is a prerequisite for attaining success in life because doing so, you are in harmony with your conscience and hence with the never-ending stretch of time. And, being this eternal force of nature in your control, how can success dare not to enter and stay in your life forever?

Now let's ponder upon the other two questions, i.e., where to begin and how to go about it. As I said, one must begin where one is standing presently; this implies that one must begin in the circumstances one is surrounded by and with as many resources as one possesses in his pocket. In other words, one must never be complaining of or holding the circumstances and lack of resources as a cause for not being able to achieve success in life. This is because both these factors are, undoubtedly, under one's control if only one is determined, dedicated and devoted to attaining success in life.

Conclusion

The kick start of your success lies in the present moment. Thus, it is required on your part to stay awake, live each moment to brimful and continue to hunt for the starting point to your success trip, for every moment contains in itself endless opportunities and once you begin to seek it, you will realize quite soon that the most apt onset to your success is now, with whatever you have, wherever you are.

XXIV

the theory of X-ray

How would you react on seeing the very first x-ray report in your life? While it would be nearly impossible for you to understand the intricacies, I guess you would be frightened or rather enthralled to know what kind of complexities find way into the internal structure of your body. In quite a same way, my dear readers, success brings with itself a basketful of emotions, perplexities, accolades, downfalls, and a mixture of wanted and unwanted events; and you can't afford turning a blind eye to any of these.you need to see through and scan each and everything that comes your way in any shape, size or form, resembling the task of an x-ray machine, for each one of these carries its own unique significance in your success story – not only do they make you aware of the path you are walking on but also enable you to explore the true meaning of success. As an x-ray of a body part enables the doctor to diagnose the ailment in the part and hence prescribe its cure, in quite a similar way, x-ray of your efforts towards success facilitates the diagnosis of their effectiveness thereby ensuring that the efforts taken by you be not in vain but worthy and fruitful and productive enough. No doubt, each and every effort may not directly give you a specific result or advantage that you seek, still it is pretty much required for you to ensure that each effort be synchronized and not deviated but in harmony with your chief goal. Thus, you must conduct a detailed analysis, somewhat similar to a SWOT analysis in business studies (analysis of strengths, weaknesses, opportunities and threats for a business enterprise) of whatever you face throughout your journey. People say not to leave any stone unturned; I say – leave no pebble unanalyzed that sits on your way to success. As I aforesaid in "the theory of odds to favor" that it is among the painful thorns that you will find the roses of greatest opportunities, hence analyzing not only the gigantic difficulties but each and every pebble you come across while heading for success is desirable. This analysis is, again, not a single but a multistep process, which involves sorting i.e., distinguishing each step from others, studying its prefix and suffix i.e., causes and implications, and, if found unfavorable, substituting it with a favorable one.

Conclusion

As philosophers in all the ages have proposed that the best way to do away with a bad habit is to replace it with a good one, and to inculcate a good habit you need to practice it for 21 days consistently. The same principle, my dear readers, applies in the world of success as well. Preparing an X-ray report each little step taken and then replacing the unfavorable ones with the favorable is extremely required. The only difference, in order to inculcate success, is that you need to practice the process of X-ray not only for 21 days but for as long as you want success to stay

in your life.

XXV

The theory of YOU (You Ought to be Unique)

People say - life's too short. I say, it's long enough and worthy merely of discovering that one idiosyncratic spark in "you" that most people remain incognizant of.let me put across a very simple yet interesting question to you - do you think being different makes any difference in your life? Yes, absolutely. In fact, being different makes a difference not only in your own life but hundreds of millions of lives around you, because when you are different, you inspire. You then prove to this world how a petty thing can be dealt with so unconventionally, or, how a common everyday thing can be looked at with so outstanding a perspective. And doing so, you are deemed to be successful - not just for your own self but many others, for you have now become a role model for them. Being different is thus a matter of pride and a mark of self-discovery.understanding this from other way round, just imagine - can you be ever inspired by a person who is just like you or like everyone else? For more clarity, let us take the example of "famous personalities". Do you think the famous personalities around you – whether it be business tycoons, film celebrities, sport champions, or star politicians exert any kind of influence on you? For sure, they do. They do influence you in some way or the other. And, the reason is, you like a peculiar attribute in them, which distinguishes them from others. And that is why, you often treat them as your role models;becauseyou want to inculcate that distinct attribute in your own self. However, in actuality, you can never be like your role models, exactly. No doubt, you can imitate their dress up, or voice, or, in short, you can imitate them to an extent, but not from tip to toe. Hence, you say that you want to be like them, because, in actuality,you are never like them. In a similar manner, my dear readers, no one can imitate you as well, for you are unique too. The only line that separates you from these famous personalities is that they are well aware of their own distinctness and you aren't. You, undoubtedly, have a unique caliber within you which you haven't discovered yet. And that is the reason why the world doesn't know who the real you is. Thus,in order to make others proud of your unique self, you need to explore and take pride in it, in the first place. Once you do so, my dear readers, it's not a long way before the world knows how unique you are, and takes pride in it too. And when that happens, you see, as i aforesaid – you are deemed to be successful.

Conclusion

The key that this chapter provides is - you are unique and you must embrace this fact. Instead of following the

footfalls of other, no matter however celebrated he or she be, tread on a path of your choice, independent of everyone else than you. Remember always that you have got that power in you which no one else exactly has, and you are the one who is the most suitable to direct it. So, what are you waiting for? Get up and look into the mirror – your role model is standing right in front of you. Now emulate all the traits you want from this role model standing in front of your eyes.

XXVI

the theory of Zenith

You all want to be on the top of the world, above all heights and right below the very first layer of sky, like a diamond shining high and brightest of bright, right? To reach there, one needs to mount a ladder but to be there and not to fall like a shooting missile, one needs to build one's own floor, tile by tile. You all want to be a plane taking off and never landing again and never crashing in the sky either. To fly like that, one needs strengthened wings but to remain intact, one needs to balance the self, inch by inch.you all want to see the far end of the tunnel without passing through the troublesome funnel, like a magic carpet carrying you from starting point to destination with no jerk. To witness the end, one needs to walk a million ton but to escape the dark and not lose hope, one needs a consistent ray of light, if not the sun. In other words, my dear readers, the true meaning of success lies in perseverance, balancing yourself rather than inclining, and, enlightening yourself all through. The essence of success is not just grabbing it once but holding it tight to your heart forever. Thus, if you seek not to touch the zenith and find your way back to the ground, but to be on par with it for all times to come; remember –

"Reaching the destiny is not thy end, but living the destiny is thy purpose.

Making money is not thy objective, but receiving riches is thy honor.

Empty mindedness is not thy characteristic, but eagerness to invite thoughts is thy custom.

Generating difficulties is not thy task, but embracing it is thy duty.

Finding what thee seek is thy fortune, but volunteering to search for it is thy choice.

Designing the Destiny is his deed, but writing your own is thy style."

EPILOGUE

Success is neither a train journey (a specific process one must undertake) nor a station you desire to arrive at (the end you seek). It is omnipresent (present everywhere). It is right there in you, with you, around you, above your head, below your feet, within your hands, and, without a blink. It is just that, as i aforesaid, that you have got a blurred pair of glasses, a pair which doesn't fit your eyes and the extent of your vision. It is desirable thus that you change your glasses and not your vision.

Now that you have come to the end of this book, i am quite sure that you must have been able to unblur your vision thereby making yourself ready to make an eye contact with the figure called "success", without any fail or misunderstanding (i.e., making it "sucking" instead of "success").

I hereby wish you a good luck for all yourface-to-face encounters with success awaiting your life ahead.

Printed by Libri Plureos GmbH in Hamburg, Germany